D1539260

Careers without College

Surgical Technician

by E. Russell Primm

Consultant:

Kevin B. Frey, CST, B.A.

Education Coordinator

Association of Surgical Technologists, Inc.

CAPSTONE BOOKS

an imprint of Capstone Press
Mankato, Minnesota

Capstone Books are published by Capstone Press
151 Good Counsel Drive, P.O. Box 669, Mankato, Minnesota 56002
http://www.capstone-press.com

Library of Congress Cataloging-in-Publication Data
Primm, E. Russell, 1958–
    Surgical technician/by E. Russell Primm.
    p. cm.--(Careers without college)
    Summary: Outlines the educational requirements, duties, salary, employment
outlook, and possible future positions of surgical technologists.
    ISBN 1-56065-709-X
    1. Surgical technology--Vocational guidance--Juvenile literature. [1. Surgical
technology--Vocational guidance. 2. Vocational guidance.]
I. Title. II. Series: Careers without college (Mankato, Minn.)
RD32.3.P75 1998
617'.0233--DC21

                                                    97–32085
                                                    CIP
                                                    AC

Photo credits:
International Stock, 19; Julian Cotton, cover; Michael J. Howell, 14;
    Bill Stanton, 22; Frank Grant, 25; Jay Thomas, 30; Greg Voight, 39
Leslie O'Shaughnessy, 11, 12, 20, 36, 46
Photo Network, 17, 45; Larry Dunmire, 35; Esbin-Anderson, 4; Tom
    McCarthy, 43; Stock Imagery, 6
James L. Shaffer, 28
Valan Photos/Dr. A. Farquhar, 9, 32; Ken Patterson, 26

Table of Contents

Note to readers:
According to the Association of Surgical Technologists, the title of this occupation is changing from surgical technician to surgical technologist. The Dictionary of Occupational Titles, however, currently lists this occupation as surgical technician.

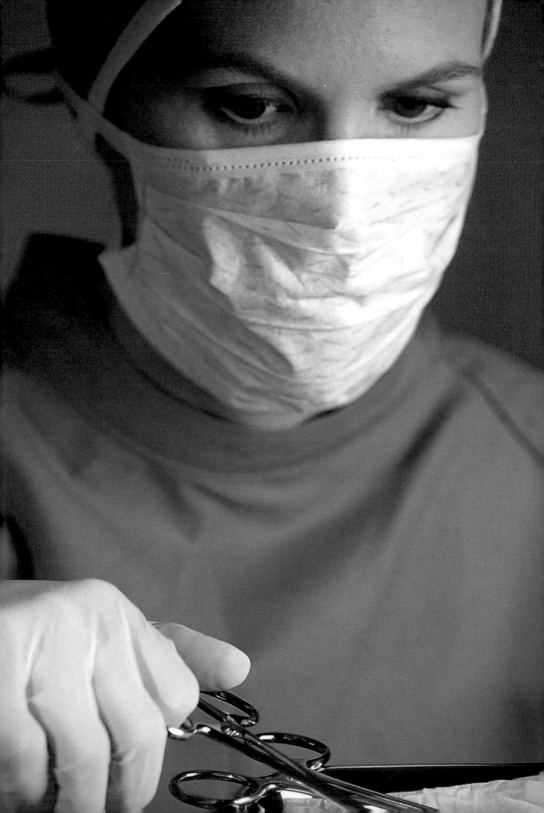

Fast Facts

Career Title _____ Surgical Technician

Minimum Educational
Requirement _____ Graduation from a
formal program

Certification Requirement _____ Recommended

U.S. Salary Range _____ $19,760 to $29,100

Canadian Salary Range _____ $20,100 to $47,800
(Canadian dollars)

U.S. Job Outlook _____ Much faster than the average

Canadian Job Outlook _____ Much faster than the average

DOT Cluster _____ Professional, technical, and
(Dictionary of Occupational Titles) managerial occupations

DOT Number —————————— 079.374-022

GOE Number _____ 10.03.02
(Guide for Occupational Exploration)

NOC _____ 3219
(National Occupational Classification—Canada)

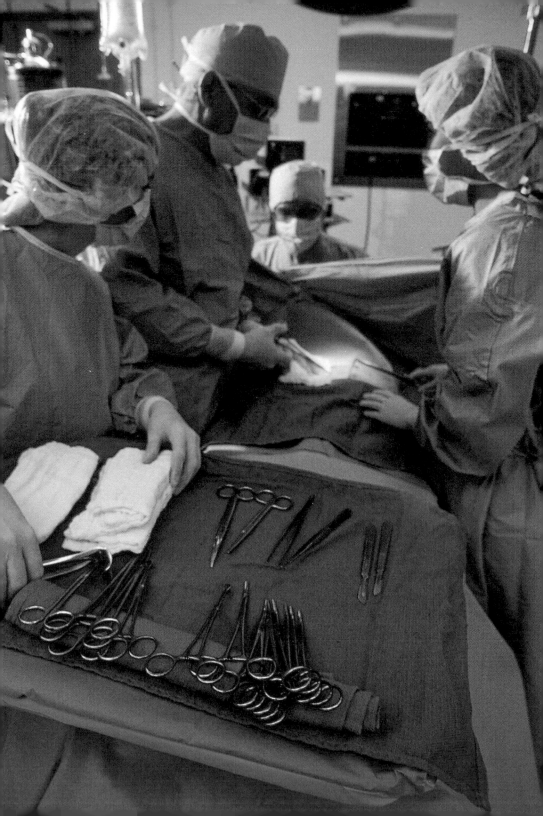

Chapter 1

Job Responsibilities

Surgical technicians assist doctors before, during, and after surgery. Surgery is repairing or removing parts of the body that are sick or hurt. Surgical technicians are also called surgical technologists.

Surgical technicians are an important part of medical teams. Surgical technicians prepare patients for surgery. They also assist in operating rooms.

Surgical technicians assist doctors before, during, and after surgery.

Surgical Teams

Surgical technicians work in surgical teams. A surgical team is a group of skilled medical workers. Each person on a team performs certain tasks during surgery. Surgeons perform operations. Assistants help the surgeons cut the patient's skin and muscle. Anesthetists give the patient gas or medicine to prevent pain during surgery. Nurses keep track of the patient's condition.

Surgical technicians prepare patients for surgery. During surgeries, they hand tools to surgeons and keep track of supplies. They clean tools after surgeries.

Preparing for Surgery

Doctors perform most surgeries in operating rooms. Surgical technicians prepare operating rooms before surgeries. They collect surgical supplies. They open packages of sponges and needles. They make sure the surgeon's tools are

Surgical technicians keep track of tools and supplies during surgeries.

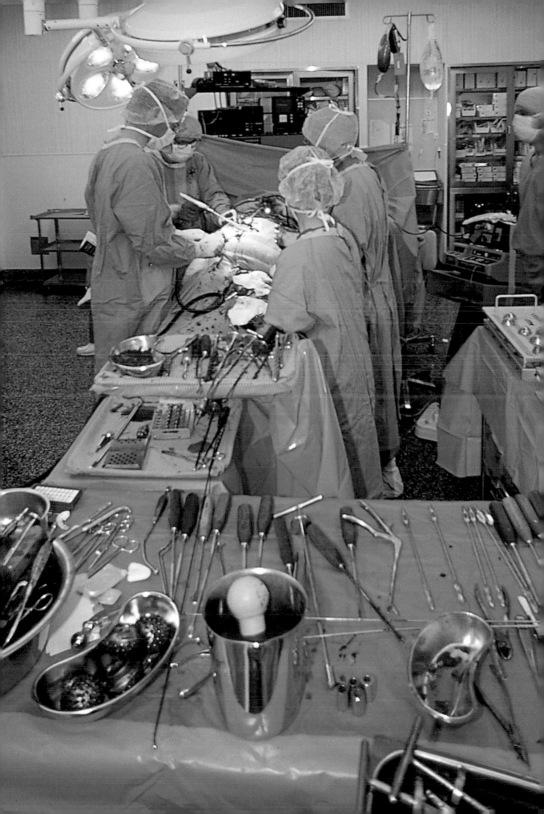

sterile. Sterile means free of germs and dirt. Tools that are not sterile can cause infection. Infection is a sickness caused by germs.

Surgical technicians also prepare patients for surgery. They talk to patients and help them stay calm. They shave patients' bodies in places where surgeons plan to cut. This keeps hair from getting into the cuts. They also clean these places by rubbing or pouring an antiseptic on them. Antiseptics kill germs and prevent infection.

Roles During Surgery

Surgical technicians often serve as scrub persons during surgery. Scrub persons set up the sterile field. A sterile field is the area around the patient that must remain free of germs.

The surgical team must wear sterile gowns, gloves, and masks. Surgical technicians help doctors put on sterile gowns, gloves, and masks.

A scrub person must not touch anything that is not sterile. Surgical technicians must watch every

Surgical technicians prepare patients for surgery.

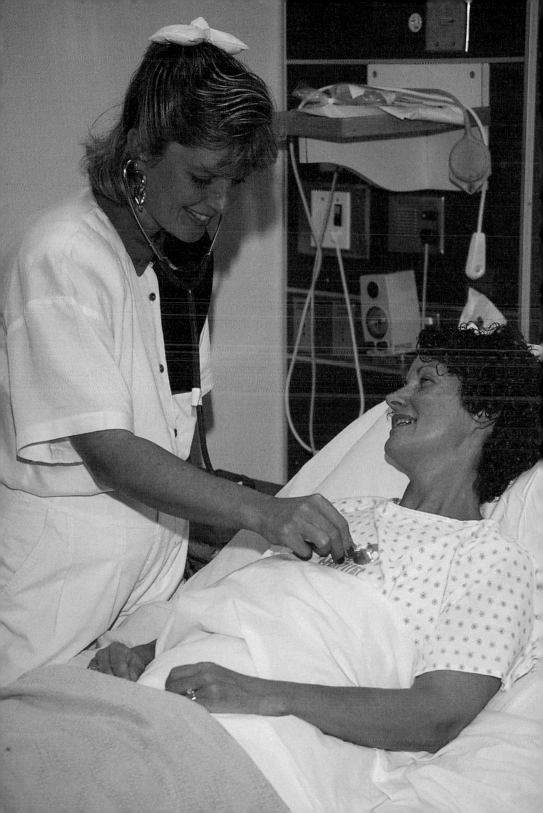

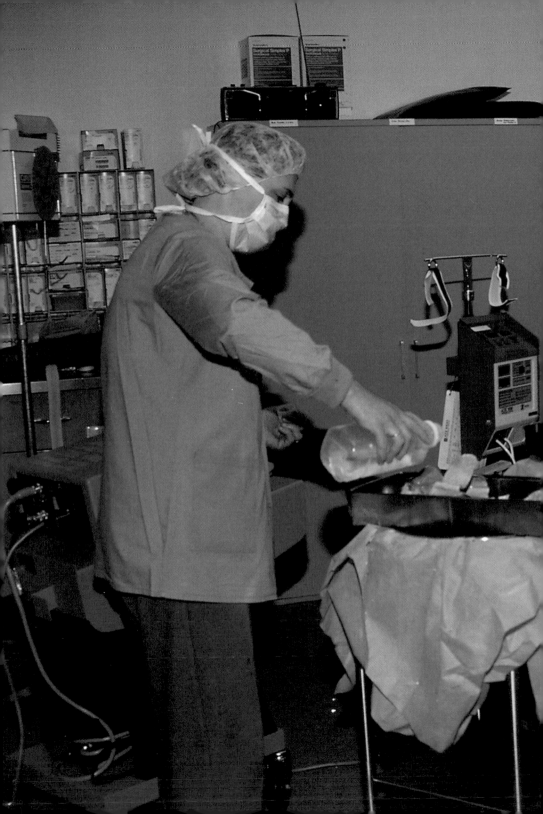

person in the operating room. They must be ready to help as they are needed. Surgeons may call in another surgical technician if they need extra help.

Surgical technicians hand tools to surgeons as the surgeons work. The technicians also keep track of all needles and sponges used during surgery. They make sure surgeons do not leave these objects inside the patient by accident.

Surgical technicians sometimes serve as circulators during surgeries. Circulators move around the sterile field. Circulators do not wear sterile gloves. They do not touch patients or any tools that will touch patients. They watch surgeries and take notes. Sometimes surgeons need extra supplies. Circulators get them.

Surgical technicians put bandages or casts on patients after surgeries. Most surgical technicians also clean operating rooms after surgeries.

Surgical technicians sometimes serve as circulators during surgery.

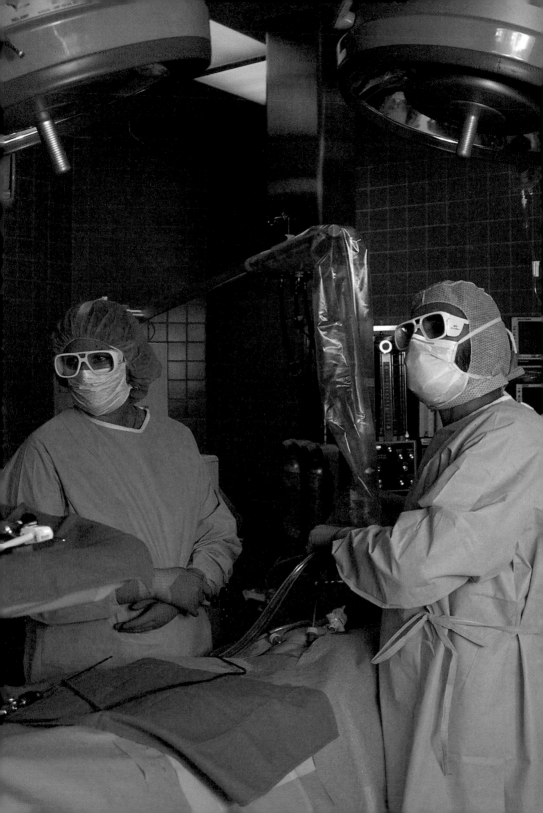

Chapter 2

What the Job Is Like

Surgical technicians spend most of their time in operating rooms. Operating rooms are clean and cool. They are also well-lighted.

Surgical technicians must wear sterile gowns, gloves, caps, and masks. Most technicians also wear plastic glasses or goggles. The goggles protect their eyes from blood, body fluids, and sharp instruments.

Surgical technicians must wear sterile gowns, gloves, caps, and masks.

Surgeries can last a long time. Surgical technicians must stand for hours at a time. They must pay attention at all times.

Surgical technicians must work well under tense situations. Surgery can be very stressful. Surgery can mean life or death for the patient. Surgeries do not always go as planned. A patient may bleed too much. Sometimes a patient's heart stops. Surgical teams must work quickly to save the patient when these things happen.

Working Conditions

Most surgical technicians work at least 40 hours per week. Many work more than 40 hours per week. Surgical technicians can earn more money by working extra hours.

Surgical technicians work different hours. Surgical technicians work during the day most of the time. Most surgeries are performed during the day. Sometimes surgical technicians work at

Surgical technicians must stand for hours at a time.

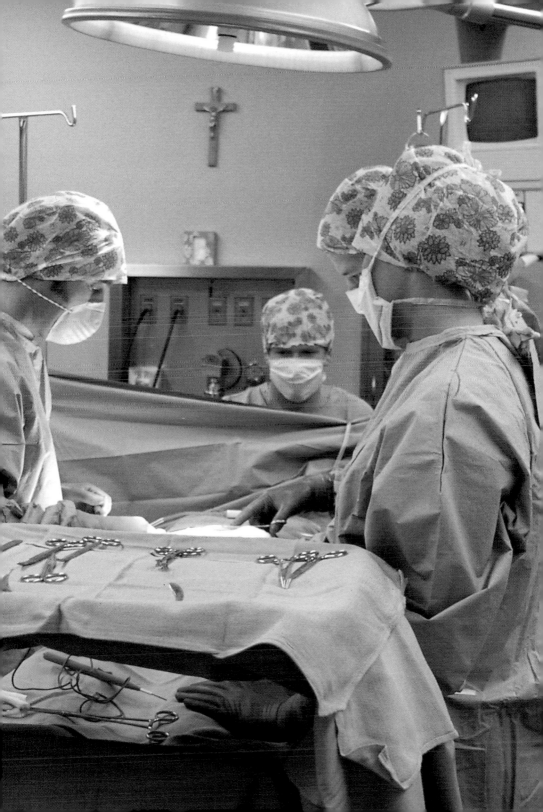

night or on weekends. Patients need care at night and on weekends, too.

Surgical technicians are sometimes on call for emergency surgeries. Emergency surgeries are not planned. They must be performed quickly to save very sick or seriously hurt patients. Surgical technicians who are on call must be ready to rush to hospitals at any time.

Sometimes the conditions in hospitals are difficult. Surgical technicians may smell odors and see unpleasant sights. Patients may be difficult to work with because of their illnesses. Technicians are sometimes exposed to contagious diseases. Contagious means easily spread.

Important Traits

Surgical technicians or technologists should have certain traits. A trait is a quality that makes people different from each other. Surgical technicians must want to help people. They must

Surgical technicians must be able to work well under tense situations.

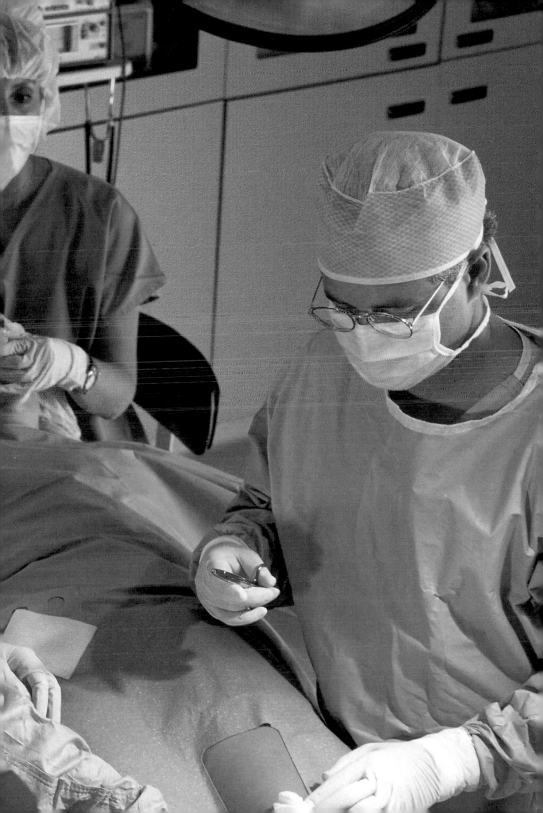

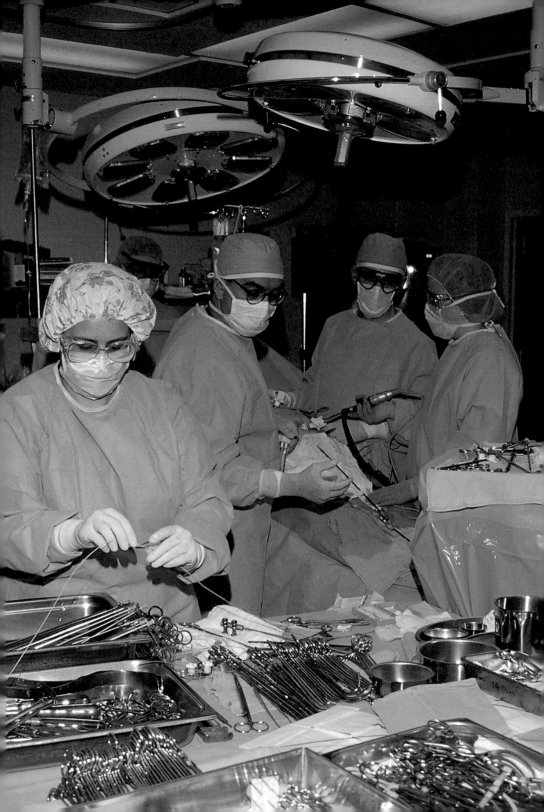

care about others. They must be able to talk calmly to patients.

Surgical technicians should be able to work around blood. People who feel ill or faint when they see blood should consider other kinds of work.

Surgical technicians also must be able to work for long periods of time under difficult situations. They should be able to stand for many hours. Surgical technicians also should be able to stay focused for hours at a time. They should be able to work quickly without making mistakes.

Surgical technicians find satisfaction in their work because they play an important role. Their help is vital before, during, and after surgeries.

Surgical technicians' help is vital before, during, and after surgeries.

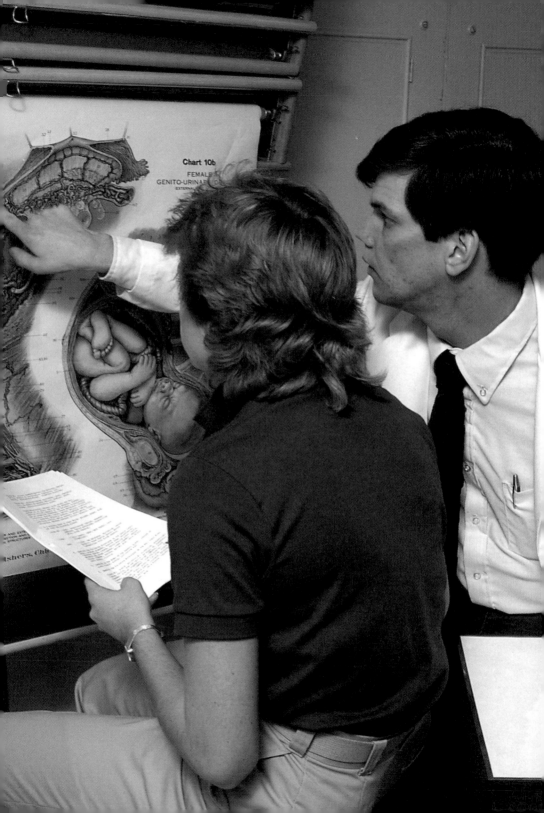

Chapter 3

Training

People who want to be surgical technicians must finish high school. After high school, they may study at junior colleges, hospitals, or in the military. They study surgical technology. Most surgical technology programs last nine or 12 months. A few programs are two years long.

Students in surgical technology programs take anatomy classes.

What Surgical Technicians Learn

Surgical technology programs include classes and clinical experience. Students take science classes such as anatomy and physiology. Anatomy is the study of the human body. Physiology is the study of how the body works. Students also learn medical terms.

Surgical technology students must complete a surgical rotation as part of their training. Surgical rotation is the time surgical technology students spend in hospitals observing surgical technicians and surgeons. They observe surgeries in operating rooms. They watch surgical technicians doing their work.

Surgical technicians also study medical ethics. An ethic is a belief in doing what is right. People who work in health care must have strong ethics. For example, doctors, nurses, and surgical technicians all believe that patients' records are private. They do not talk about patients' health

Surgical technology students observe surgeons and surgical technicians in operating rooms.

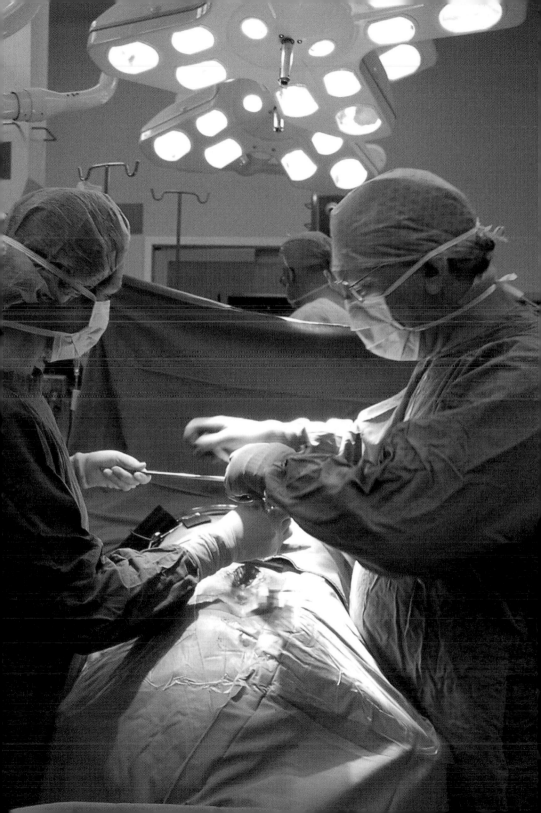

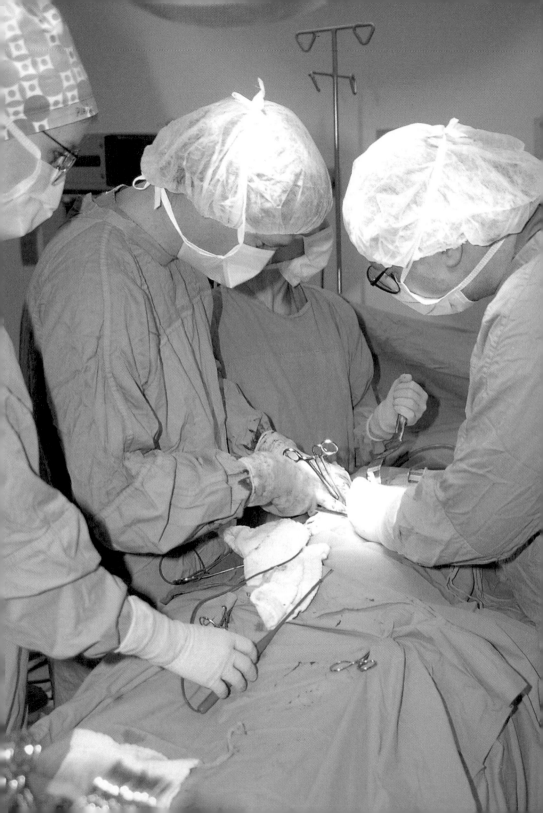

with other people. To do so would be against their ethics.

Certification

Many surgical technicians choose to become certified. Certification is an official recognition of a person's abilities and skills. Technicians must take a long test to become certified. This test asks surgical technicians many questions about their work. Only surgical technicians who are very good at their jobs can pass this test.

Surgical technicians who pass this test may use the title Certified Surgical Technologist. Most people call them CSTs. Many hospitals will not hire surgical technicians who are not CSTs.

What Students Can Do Now

Students who would like to become surgical technicians should study math and science. They also should take health classes.

Many surgical technicians become Certified Surgical Technologists.

Students who want to be surgical technicians should volunteer at hospitals or nursing homes. Volunteer means to offer to do a job without pay. Volunteer work can help students learn about the health care field. It can help students decide if they enjoy caring for people who are sick.

Students who want to be surgical technicians can volunteer to work at hospitals or nursing homes.

Students should also learn cardiopulmonary resuscitation (CPR). This is a method of restarting a heart that has stopped beating. CPR involves breathing into a person's mouth. It also involves pressing on the patient's chest in a certain rhythm.

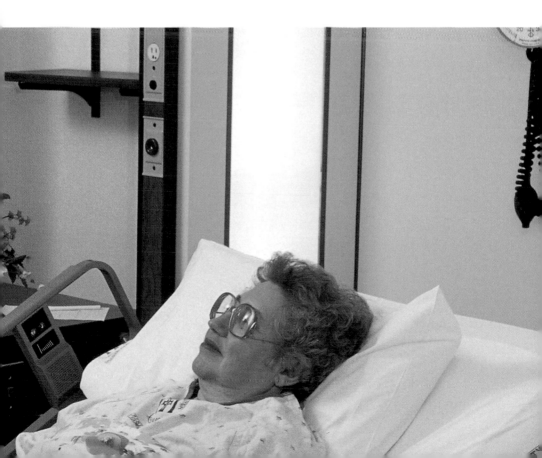

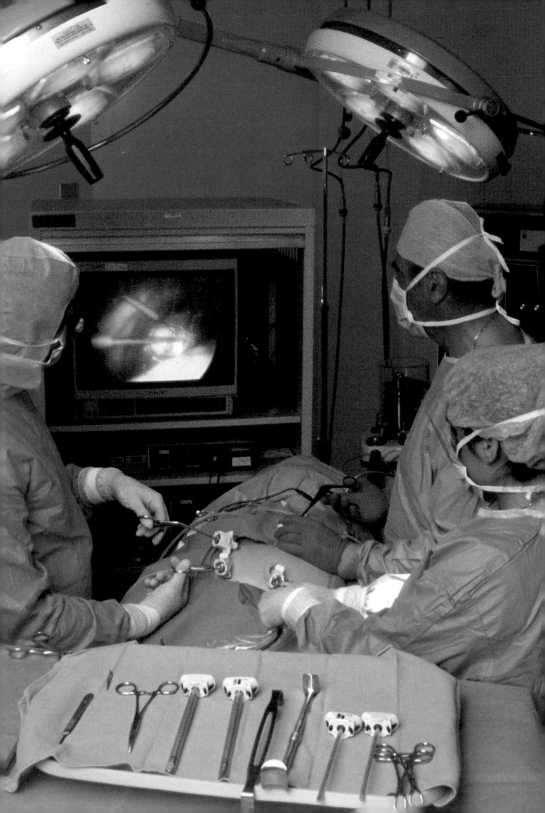

Chapter 4

Salary and Job Outlook

Surgical technology is a growing career choice in both Canada and the United States. The demand for surgical technicians is increasing. In fact, most hospitals cannot find enough people to fill these important jobs.

Surgical technology is a growing career choice.

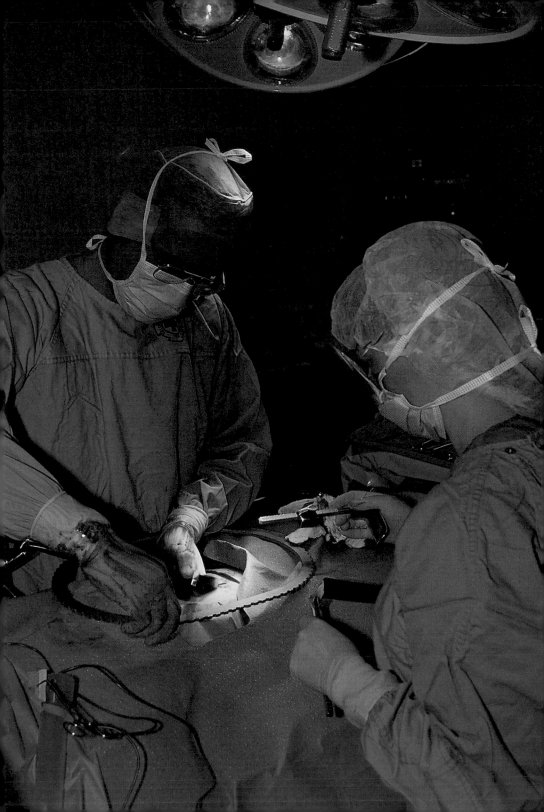

Salary

Surgical technicians' salaries depend on experience and training. In the United States and Canada, surgical technicians who have worked many years earn the most money. Those who work in private surgeons' offices usually earn more money than those who work for hospitals.

Surgical technicians with extra training also can earn higher salaries. CSTs earn more money than other surgical technicians.

Surgical technicians in the United States can earn from $19,760 to $29,100. Most earn about $22,000. Surgical technicians in Canada can earn from $20,100 to $47,800. Most surgical technicians in Canada earn about $33,500.

Surgical technicians with extra training can earn higher salaries.

Job Outlook

Surgical technology will continue to grow in coming years. The need for surgical technicians is growing because more surgeries are being performed. This is true for many reasons.

More people live in the United States and Canada than ever before. Surgeons perform more surgeries because there are more people. People also live longer than they used to. Older people need more surgeries than younger people. Doctors learn more every year. They can perform new surgeries to save lives. Surgeons need more surgical technicians to help them perform all these surgeries.

Surgeons need surgical technicians to help them perform surgeries.

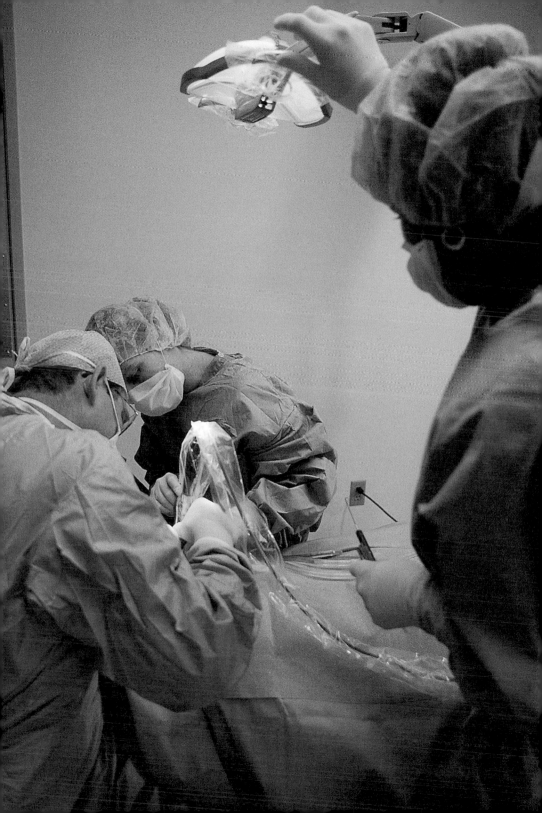

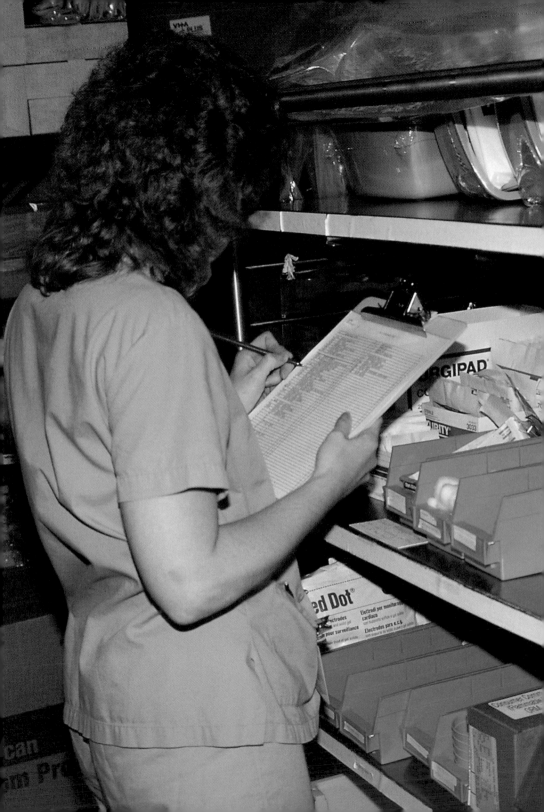

Chapter 5

Where the Job Can Lead

Surgical technicians can find many ways to advance in their careers. They can take on more responsibilities. Some surgical technicians schedule surgeries and order supplies. Others manage surgical technicians. These people earn more than surgical technicians who work only in operating rooms.

Some surgical technicians order supplies.

Training on the Job
Surgical technicians also can advance by learning more health care skills. Those who can do more jobs within hospitals will earn more money. Some may learn to give patients emergency care such as CPR.

Other surgical technicians learn to give patients special tests. They may use needles to collect blood samples. Others may use machines to check patients' hearts.

Advanced Training
Some surgical technicians advance by becoming surgical first assistants after they complete additional training. Surgical first assistants help surgeons work on the patient's body. They use tools to pull back the patient's skin while surgeons work. They use sponges to soak up blood so surgeons can see inside the patient's body.

Surgical technicians may also advance by seeking new health care jobs. They may become nurses or doctors. Nurses and doctors must study medicine for many years.

Surgical first assistants help surgeons work on patients' bodies.

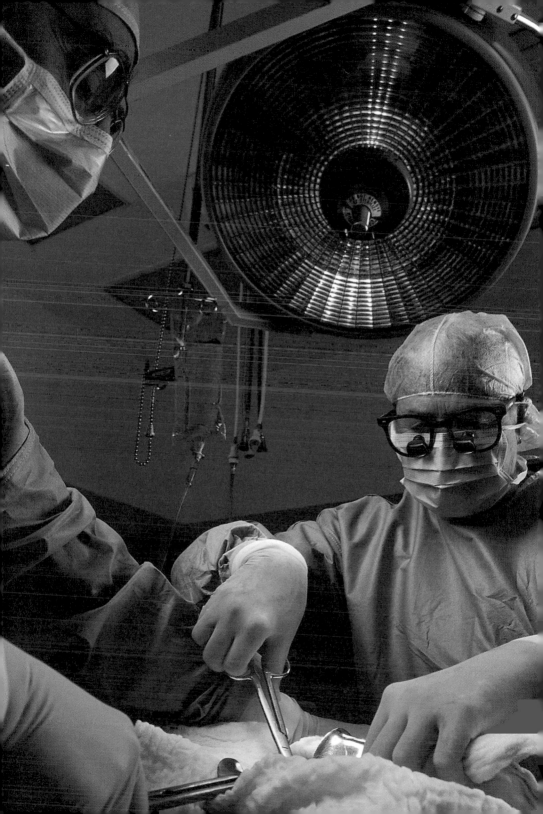

Words to Know

anatomy (uh-NAT-uh-mee)—the study of the human body

antiseptic (an-ti-SEP-tik)—something that kills germs and prevents infection

biology (bye-OL-uh-jee)—the study of living things

cardiopulmonary resuscitation (kar-dee-oh-PUHL-muh-nair-ee ree-se-se-TAY-shuhn)—a method of restarting a heart that has stopped beating; it involves breathing into a patient's mouth and pressing on a patient's chest in a certain rhythm; (CPR)

certification (sur-ti-fuh-KAY-shun)—an official recognition of a person's abilities and skills

contagious (kuhn-TAY-juhss)—easily spread

infection (in-FEK-shuhn)—a sickness caused by germs

physiology (fiz-ee-OL-uh-jee)—the study of how the body works

sterile (STER-uhl)—free of germs and dirt

surgeon (SUR-juhn)—a doctor who performs surgery

surgery (SUR-jer-ee)—repairing or removing parts of the body that are sick or hurt

trait (TRATE)— a quality that makes people different from each other

volunteer (vol-uhn-TIHR)—to offer to do a job without pay

To Learn More

Lee, Barbara. *Working in Health Care and Wellness*. Minneapolis: Lerner Publications Co., 1996.

Paradis, Adrian A. *Careers for Caring People and Other Sensitive Types*. Lincolnwood, Ill.: National Textbook Co., 1995.

Smith, Ronald R. *Surgical Technologist*. Smith Career Notes, 1993.

Wilkinson, Beth. *Careers Inside the World of Health Care*. New York: Rosen Publishing Group, 1995.

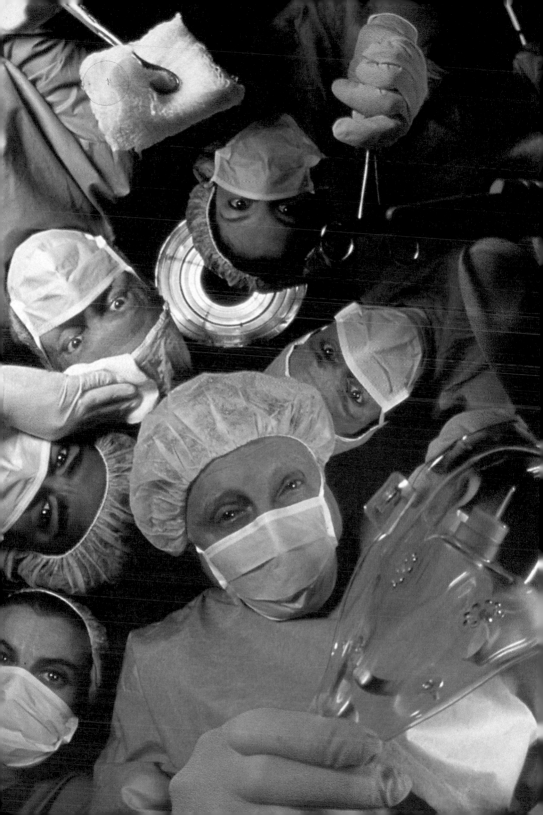

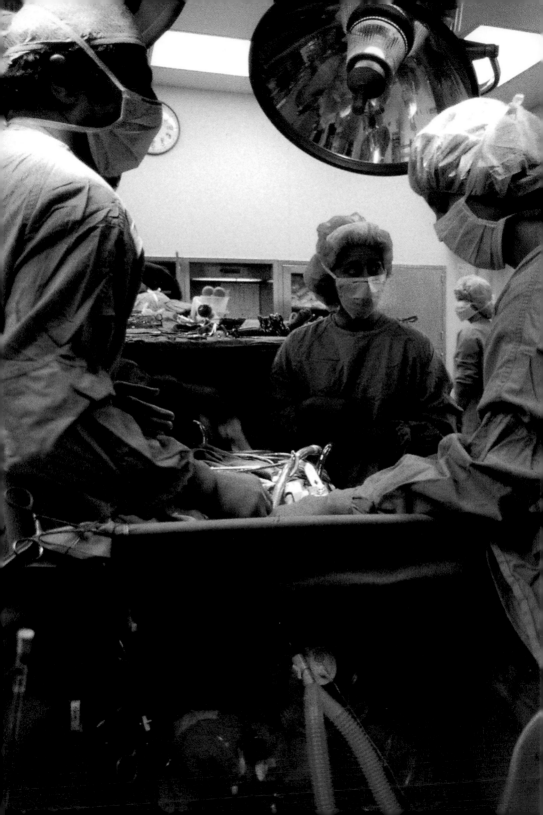

Useful Addresses

Association of Surgical Technologists, Inc. (AST)
7108-C South Alton Way, Suite 100
Englewood, CO 80112-2106

National School of Health Sciences
Bethesda, MD 20889-5611

Internet Sites

Association of Surgical Technologists
http://www.ast.org

Medical Technologists and Technicians
http://www.hrdc-drhc.gc.ca/JobFutures/
    english/volum1/321/321.htm

Surgical Technologists
http://stats.bls.gov/oco/ocos106.htm

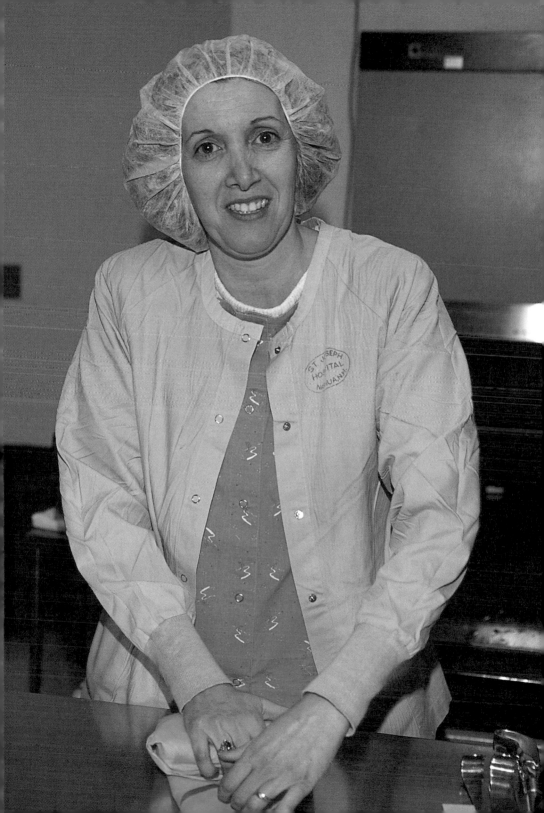

Index